THE VIKINGS

Text: **Tom Stanier** and **Harry Sutton**
Illustrations: **Peter Kesteven**

Adviser: **Richard Hall**, York Archaeological Trust.

Contents

	Pages
The Mystery Raiders	2 and 3
The Norsemen	4 and 5
Town Life	6 and 7
Viking Adventures	8 and 9
The Viking Ships	10 and 11
Westwards!	12
On to Vinland . . .	13 to 15
The Viking Gods	16
Thor's Journey	17 to 19
The Vikings and England	20 to 23
The Sea Rovers	24 and 25
Viking Britain — the end of the story	26 and 27
Our Viking Heritage	28
Jorvik	29
Model of a Viking Longship	30 and 31
Index	32

BBC Books in association with Heritage Books

The Mystery Raiders

On the island of Lindisfarne off the coast of Northumbria, there was a famous monastery. The monks lived out their lives working for God, and it seemed to them that nothing could disturb their peaceful existence. But one day, in the year 793, there came disaster. A writer at the time described the event: 'During this year,' he wrote, 'great portents appeared over Northumbria and made people sore afraid. There were violent whirlwinds and comets were seen flying through the air.'
'A serious famine followed hard on these signs and shortly after, in the same year, the heathen men cruelly laid waste to God's church in Lindisfarne.'
Who were the mystery 'heathens' who attacked the helpless monks in Lindisfarne? And where had they come from?
This book tells their story.

The Norsemen

The raiders who appeared so mysteriously at Lindisfarne, came from Scandinavia. These lands, which are made up of the modern countries of Norway, Sweden and Denmark, are north of Britain and the people of Scandinavia were called Norse(north)men. They were also known as 'Vikings'. Although they appeared so fearsome to the monks of Lindisfarne, most of the Vikings who manned the longships to raid abroad, lived peaceful lives at home in Scandinavia. On these two pages you can see how many of them were farmers and fishermen, living peacefully in the country and by the sea.

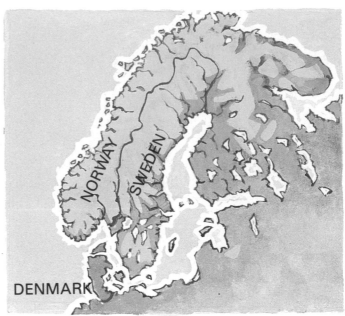

1 This is a map of Scandinavia — the homelands of the Vikings.

2 The landscape of Scandinavia is very varied. On the west coast (modern Norway), there are sea inlets called fjords and very high cliffs. Sea birds nested in the cliffs and their eggs were often collected for food.

3 To the east (modern Sweden), the land is flatter and there are many islands close to the shore. These gave safe channels to ships where they were sheltered from gales and rough seas. The seas round the coasts abounded with fish.

4 Denmark, (in the south), is flatter still with very few trees. It is good farming land and the Viking farmers used to grow barley, rye, wheat, oats and vegetables such as peas and beans.

5 Houses were made of material found locally. The farming settlement in the picture is in Denmark where houses were made of wood.

DRINKING VESSEL

SPOON

SCOOP

LADLE

PLATE

6 Farmers lived in longhouses with their animals living at one end during the winter. There was a long, stone-paved fireplace down the middle of the earth floor, and a low wooden platform along each side, where the people would sit in daytime and sleep at night.

In this picture a rich farmer is dining with his family. Meat was roasted over the fire on a spit (1), or boiled in a cauldron (2) with vegetables. The tools needed for cooking, scoops (3), bowls (4) and tubs for holding flour, milk, etc. (5), were made of wood.

5

Town Life

Most Vikings lived in the country as farmers, but there were also craftsmen such as blacksmiths, weavers, silversmiths and carpenters. All these people needed places in which to live and work and also markets where they could display and sell their goods. They found what they needed by living together in towns which had walls round them for protection from robbers.

1 Viking towns were always sited near the sea because merchants needed ships for trading. There were a few roads along which traders could travel, but these were mostly tracks for farmers to drive their cattle to market. The towns had gates in their walls through which travellers had to pass. These entrances were closed and guarded at night.

2 The Vikings made very good cloth for clothes and for the sails of their ships. Many homes had looms, like the one in the picture.

3 There was only one room inside this merchant's house, but it was warm and cosy.

4 The shops in Viking towns were mostly stalls set up in the street. In this picture you can see the stalls of a jeweller, a shoe-seller and an antler-carver.

5 There were other craftsmen — potters, carpenters, bronze workers, blacksmiths, and many more. But it is the Viking shipbuilders who are best remembered. The word 'Viking' is thought to mean 'roving' and if they had not known how to build fine, seaworthy ships, the Vikings would not have been able to go 'roving' across the seas.

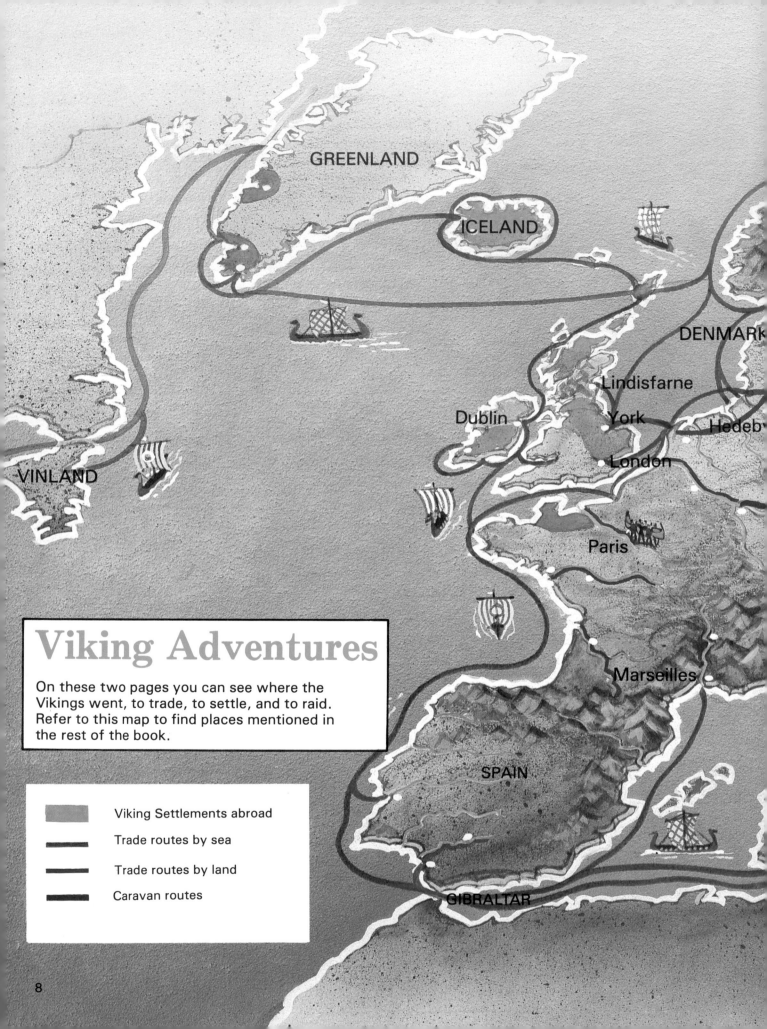

GREENLAND

ICELAND

DENMARK

Lindisfarne

Dublin

York

Hedeby

London

VINLAND

Paris

Marseilles

SPAIN

Viking Adventures

On these two pages you can see where the
Vikings went, to trade, to settle, and to raid.
Refer to this map to find places mentioned in
the rest of the book.

Viking Settlements abroad

Trade routes by sea

Trade routes by land

Caravan routes

GIBRALTAR

NORWAY

SWEDEN

Uppsala

Trelleborg

Bulgar

Kiev

CASPIAN SEA

BLACK SEA

Constantinople

Rome

Baghdad

Salerno

MEDITERRANEAN SEA

The Viking Ships

Many Vikings lived close to rivers, lakes, islands and fjiords (sea inlets), and they grew up from childhood able to row and sail all kinds of boats. For centuries, ships had been used for fishing, for travel, and for carrying goods. They were specially designed for each purpose. Nowhere in Europe were there faster ships or more skilled sailors.

In this picture you can see a Viking longship at sea. The people on board are starting out on a long voyage. All the things they will need for the journey are stowed on board. Notice the casks for water (1); the sea chests for their belongings, which they sit on when rowing (2); the cattle and horses (3) and the rest of the cargo on board (4).

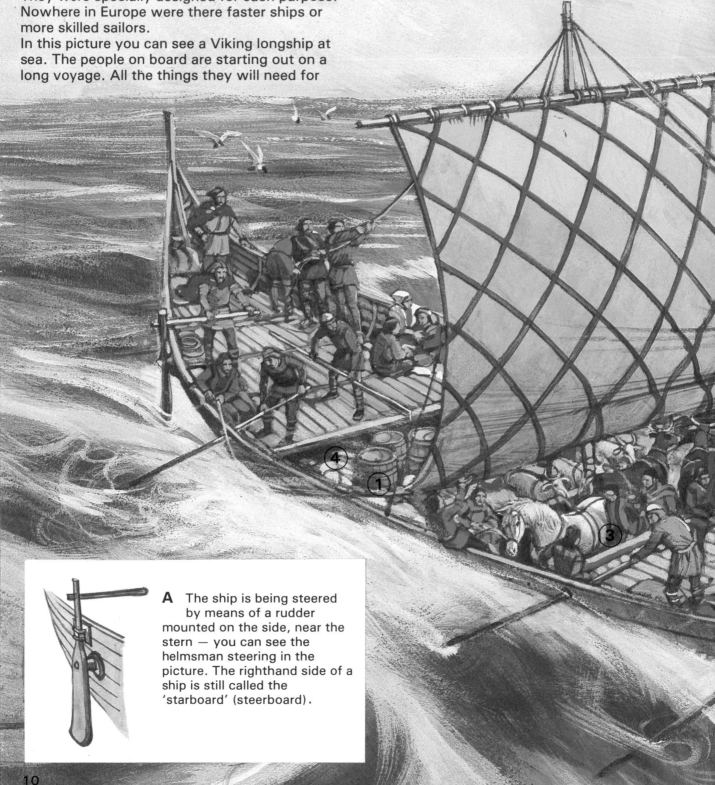

A The ship is being steered by means of a rudder mounted on the side, near the stern — you can see the helmsman steering in the picture. The righthand side of a ship is still called the 'starboard' (steerboard).

B The mast of this ship was about 10m tall and the sail was fixed to a yard about 11m long.

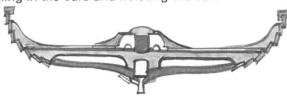

C These big ships (this one would have been about 23m long) had a very shallow draught. Even with a cargo weighing ten tons, it could have sailed in water less than 1.3m deep. They have just rowed out of harbour. Now they are pulling in the oars and hoisting the sail.

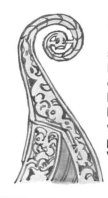

D The Vikings loved to decorate some of their ships with fine carvings. This beautiful figurehead was carved on the prow of a vessel known as the 'Oseberg ship', because that is the place where it was found. It was probably the state ship of a Viking king or lord.

Westwards!

This is the story of Viking adventures across the Atlantic Ocean. We know about them because the stories were written down, many years after they happened, by Viking story tellers. The books they wrote were called 'sagas'.

1 A thousand miles from Norway lay the empty island of Iceland. The first Viking to settle there was called Ingolfur. He brought with him the wooden pillars of his old house. He threw them overboard and swore to make his home at whatever place they washed ashore. He named his new settlement Reykjavik.

2 Within sixty years, there were 10,000 people living in Iceland. They began to hold a yearly assembly, called an 'Althing'. This is believed to be the oldest Parliament in Europe.

3 In 1000 AD, the Althing voted that the people of Iceland should become Christians. A volcano erupted nearby while they were holding the meeting. Some said that this was a warning from the old pagan gods, but the Icelanders still voted to take up the new religion.

4 In spite of the new religion, there was still plenty of fighting amongst the Icelanders. According to the sagas, when there was a blood feud, it was often settled by a duel. The two opponents would take a boat to a small island. There, a 'fight ring' would be marked out by laying a large square of cloth and fixing it to the ground with wooden pegs. If one of the fighters stepped outside the ring, he was said to have retreated and lost the fight.

5 Those who killed other people in blood feuds were often sentenced to banishment. This happened to a man called Erik the Red who was exiled for three years. He sailed off to explore a huge island to the west which was a harsh place, wild and cold. Erik called it 'Greenland' to make it sound more pleasant.

On to Vinland . . .

1 America was discovered by a Viking called Bjarne. He had been trying to sail from Iceland to Greenland, but was blown off course. Bjarne did not try to land, but when he got back to Greenland told the settlers there of what he had found.

2 Erik the Red was getting too old for voyages, but his son, Leif the Lucky was happy to set sail. He was determined to find the new country and make a landing. Perhaps Erik envied his son as he said goodbye to Leif at the shore.

3 On arrival, they found that the new country was a much more pleasant place than Greenland. There were no frosts, the grass was green and juicy and there were even wild grapes growing there.

4 They also noticed that, compared with Greenland, the days were shorter in summer and longer in winter. The new land they had discovered must therefore have been further south than Greenland. They named it 'Vinland' (Wineland), and then headed back home.

5 On the way they spotted some shipwrecked people clinging to rocks. Lief rescued them and took them back to Greenland. One of the lucky people to be saved was called Gudrid. She was a beautiful Norwegian woman and this was to be the first of many adventures for her.

6 Gudrid lived for some time at the house of Erik the Red, and one Christmas, Erik had a visitor — a ship's captain called Karlsefni. It was a Christmas to remember, for Karlsefni fell in love with Gudrid and they were married.

7 While he was staying with Erik, Karlsefni heard about Vinland. He liked the sound of it, and so did Gudrid. They determined to try to settle there and loaded their ship with pigs and sheep. They also took with them a big, black bull — which was to prove important to them, as will be seen.

8 Among the crew were two Scottish slaves — a man called Haki and a woman called Hekja. They were said to run faster than deer, and Karlsefni put them ashore at Vinland with instructions to run as far as they could in three days and see what they could find. After three days, the two of them came running back to the shore. One was carrying some wheat and the other, a bunch of wild grapes. 'This is a land of plenty', they said.

9 The Vikings were pleased with their new home and soon settled in. In the autumn they had another reason to celebrate for Gudrid gave birth to a son who was named, Snorri. This was the first European child ever to be born in North America.

10 A group of Indians arrived, anxious to trade. They brought furs, and in return they wanted some of the Vikings' red cloth. The Vikings offered them milk — something they had never before tasted.

11 All was going well when, suddenly, the bull roared. The Indians fled in panic, for they had never seen a bull. Perhaps these strange white people were not so friendly after all, they thought.

12 Next time, the Indians returned with a fleet of canoes, determined to drive the pale-skinned invaders away from their shores. It was a woman called Freydis who won the day for the Vikings. Although she was very soon to have a baby, she wielded a sword as well as any man, and routed the Indians.

13 Gudrid and Karlsefni were sad when at last they decided to leave Vinland.

14 But Gudrid's travels were far from over. A few years earlier she had become a Christian and now she decided to go on a pilgrimage to Rome. Imagine what she must have felt as she stood before the great cathedral. What a contrast with her years in Vinland!

15 From Rome, Gudrid returned to live with her son in Iceland. By now Snorri had grown up and was a farmer. He had also built a church — something that must have pleased his mother.

16 Gudrid ended her days as a nun, loved and respected by all. What stories she must have had to tell!

The Viking Gods

The Vikings believed in many gods. The King of their Gods was named Odin. He was the God of War and of Wisdom. He is usually shown with only one eye because he drank from a magic well to achieve wisdom and, in order to do this, he had to agree to sacrifice one eye. Odin had an eight-legged horse called Sleipnir on which he used to ride through the sky. He had also two ravens called Thought and Memory. Every morning he would send them off to fly through the world and find out everything that was happening. In the evening they would return to Odin and, perched on his shoulder, they would tell him all that they had seen. The word 'Wednesday' means 'Odin's Day'.

Odin's oldest son was called Thor, and he was the best loved of all the Viking gods. He was immensely strong and had a fiery hammer which he used to hurl at his enemies. Miraculously, the hammer would always come flying back to Thor and he would catch it in his iron gloves. When Vikings saw a flash of lightning, they would say that Thor had been hurling his hammer again. The Vikings liked Thor because he was a great fighter, and was very fond of eating and drinking. He would sometimes eat a whole ox and drink three barrels of mead at one sitting. The word Thursday means 'Thor's Day'.

Thor's mother was Frigga, the Goddess of Fertility and Mother of All. She used to spin gold thread on her jewelled spinning wheel and then weave it into summer clouds. The word Friday means 'Frigga's Day'.

There were many other Gods and they all lived together in a place called Asgard. Humans lived in a different world — Midgard — and there was a rainbow bridge between Asgard and Midgard which only the gods were allowed to use. There was also a race of giants, who were deadly rivals of the gods. One day, Odin's faithful ravens brought him news that the Giants were planning to cross the Rainbow Bridge and invade the Kingdom of the Gods. Odin appointed his son Heimdall, to be the Guardian of the Bridge and he warned invaders that Heimdall had wonderful hearing and sight. He could see as well at night as by day, and his ears were so sharp that he could hear the sound of grass growing in the fields. He also had a famous horn which he would blow as an alarm signal. Its notes were so piercing that it could be heard throughout the world.

Odin also decided to use the bravest of humans in his fight against the Giants. Whenever there was a battle, Odin arranged that those who had died most bravely would be taken up to Asgard to recover from their wounds and live with him. The dead fighters were carried on horseback to Asgard by warrior maidens known as Valkyries. In Asgard, they lived in a great hall called Valhalla. Five hundred men could march abreast through each of its five hundred and forty doors. The rafters consisted of gigantic spears, coats of mail lined the walls like tapestries, and the roof was tiled with shields.

Their belief in Valhalla helped to make the Vikings even better fighters. They thought that if they died bravely in battle, this would guarantee them a good life in the next world. To a Viking, cowardice was just silly.

Thor's Journey

Thor was in high spirits. A new challenge — and just when things had been getting boring. He'd had enough of fighting dragons and serpents, and he was tired of pitting his strength against his fellow gods. But this time it was going to be different. Now, with two friends, he was going to try his luck in the Great Hall of the Giants!

After a month of hard travelling, they had reached their destination, and there in front of them were the massive walls of Utgard, tall as a mountain range. For a moment they gazed in awe at the giants' stronghold. Then Thor spat on his hands. He swung his hammer over his shoulder.
'Time to get down to business!' he said.

The door of the palace was open and shoulder to shoulder with his two friends, Thor marched in. 'Greetings, Giants,' he said. 'I am Thor of Asgard, and I have come to challenge you to trials of strength.'

To his dismay, the giants just roared with laughter. 'What?', said the King of the Giants. 'A little runt like you! Is this the mighty god we have heard about? You disappoint me, Thor. This will be but poor sport.'

Thor's blood began to boil. 'Enough of this jesting,' he said. 'I know what I can do. Let us see what you can do!'

'Very well,' said the Giant King. 'You choose the first contest.'

And Thor chose a drinking match.

The king beckoned to the servants and they brought a drinking horn full of mead. At first sight, it was not very impressive. Certainly it was not very broad, but it was long and narrow — so narrow that its point disappeared into the shadows at the sides. Thor raised it to his lips. He was determined to drain it to the dregs. With huge gulps and swallows, he slurped it down. He could drink any of the other gods under the table at Asgard and he was sure that he could finish off this horn in one breath. But no, when he set the horn down, breathless and panting, he was amazed to see that the level of mead had not gone down at all.

He ground his teeth in rage and grabbed the horn back for a second attempt. And this time he nearly burst with the effort. There was a pounding in his head, the hall seemed to swim before his eyes, and there was a strange salty taste in his mouth. And yet — when he set the horn down again, the liquid had hardly gone down at all. Just an inch or two.

'Oh dear!,' cried the Giant King. 'You are clearly not much of a drinker. What would you like to try now? Perhaps the trial of strength. See that cat? Just as a warm up, lift it off the ground.'

The cat in question was a giant cat, and as tall as Thor himself. But that did not bother him too much. He knew what he could do and felt quite confident. This, he felt, would be child's play.

He should have known better, however, for every time Thor gave a heave, the cat simply arched its back. And, try as he might, the best Thor could do was to make the cat lift one foot off the ground.

'Hard luck!' said the king. 'But I suppose it is rather a big cat for such a little fellow as you.' And the other giants roared with laughter.

Thor's eyes blazed with anger, like hot coals. 'I didn't come here to play with cats,' he shouted. 'Let's have some wrestling. That is a proper sport for a man.'

'Mmm . . .' mused the king. 'But who would make a suitable opponent for you? I'm not sure that you'd be a match for any of my fellow giants. But I think I know who would be just right for you. Look — behind you. Coming now, through that door.'

And when Thor turned to look, he saw an old woman. She was white-haired and frail. Her back was bent almost double, and she hobbled as she went towards him.

Thor quivered with rage. This was the biggest insult of all! 'Right', he thought. 'I'll get this old crone out of the way and then I can get down to some real wrestling.' But the moment he laid hold of her, he knew it was not going to be so easy. The old woman was strong — she was incredibly strong! And although he heaved and sweated, she did not budge an inch.

But now it was the turn of the old woman to put on the pressure. She grasped Thor in an armlock, and then, with a wrist like iron, she began to force him downwards. Thor resisted with all his strength; the veins stood out on his forehead and his eyes almost popped out of his head. But it was useless. Moments later he was down on one knee, and the old woman had won.

Next morning, Thor and his friends set off for home. After the king had escorted them out of the palace and through the gates, Thor turned to say goodbye. 'Well, King of the Giants, it pains me to say it, but you made me look pretty foolish. And it's not often I admit to that.'

'Ah,' said the king. 'Now that you are safely out of my palace , I'll let you into a secret. You did much better than you thought, Thor. In fact, you did so well that I'm never going to let you into my palace again.'

Thor looked at the king in amazement.

'You see,' continued the king, 'I've been using magic

spells to trick you! When you were drinking from the horn, you did not know that the other end of the horn was in the sea. No wonder that you could not empty it — you were trying to drink the entire ocean!'

Thor nodded his head, sadly. A lot of things were beginning to make sense.

'And why couldn't I lift the cat?' he asked.

'Because it wasn't a cat at all,' the king told him. 'That was the gigantic Midgard serpent that encircles the whole world. And you didn't do at all badly. Nobody has ever before got it to lift even one paw! We could hardly believe our eyes.'

'And the old woman?' asked Thor. 'Who was she?'

'Old grandma?' said the king. And he laughed. 'No one has ever wrestled so long with old Grandma, for she is the spirit of Old Age. And Old Age is the strongest of all. There is nobody on earth that can resist her. Sooner or later, she brings all of us to our kees!'

Then the king looked at Thor with a smile. 'I can see that you are getting angry,' he said, 'so before you can use that hammer of yours, I will make one magic spell!' And suddenly — the king vanished. And so did the walls and the palace.

Thor scowled and muttered into his beard. 'A drinking horn, a cat, and an old woman. Who could have thought they would get the better of Thor!' But then he began to cheer up. After all, he had not been disgraced. The giants had had to use magic to get the better of him. And, picking up his hammer, he turned for home.

'Come on,' he said. 'Time to get back to Asgard. We've got a good story to tell. A story fit for the gods!'

19

The Vikings and England

To the Vikings, England must have seemed an easy prey. Their first raid, on the rich monastery at Lindisfarne, had given them a taste of England's wealth — gold, silver, jewels and many Christian treasures. Now, in the years that followed that first raid, Viking fleets began to appear at places all round the coasts of England. They landed, and the people of England fled in terror from them. Nothing, it seemed, could stop the Viking raids.

1 The people of England at this time, were Anglo Saxons, who, only three hundred years earlier, had themselves conquered England from the native Britons. Most of England was divided between the four Anglo-Saxon kingdoms of Northumbria, Mercia, Wessex and East Anglia.

2 The Anglo Saxons were Christians and the power of the church was very great.

3 There was no regular army in England. When danger threatened, the king or his noblemen, could call upon their men to serve as soldiers in their own districts, but only for about forty days — and without pay. They were not well armed and, when their time was served, they would disperse back to their farms.

4 For their part, the Vikings had one very great advantage — surprise. Round the coasts of England they could land on any one of a thousand beaches and could be miles inland before the local people even knew they had arrived.

5 The first Viking leader to bring an army to invade England was a Dane named Ivar the Boneless. In the spring of the year 866, he laid seige to the walled city of York.

York was an important town in the kingdom of Northumbria. Although the defenders fought bravely, they could not resist the fierce Viking attacks. York fell and the kingdom of Northumbria surrendered to Ivar the Boneless.

6 Only one kingdom escaped the Vikings. Alfred, King of Wessex, had made peace with them. But he was wrong in thinking that the Vikings would be satisfied with the lands they had conquered. One day, in January 878, he was celebrating Twelfth Night at his court at Chippenham, when the Vikings made a surprise attack.

7 King Alfred and some of his noblemen managed to escape.

8 For a few weeks, Alfred had to hide from the Danes. There is a famous story about the time when he took refuge in a cottage, disguised as a kitchen boy. Told by the housewife to keep an eye on some cakes which were cooking before the fire, Alfred fell into deep thought about how to defeat the Vikings — and forgot all about the cakes. Smelling the burning cakes, the housewife scolded him soundly for being so careless. She had no idea that the forgetful 'kitchen boy' was really her king!

9 But King Alfred did not spend all his time in hiding. According to another story, he once disguised himself as a travelling minstrel and made his way into a Viking camp. There he wandered around, playing his lyre — and listening to plans made by the Viking chiefs for his defeat!

10 After only five months in hiding, King Alfred gathered an army and marched against the Vikings.

11 At Edington, on the Berkshire Downs, Alfred
fought a famous battle against the Vikings.
This time it was the Vikings who had to run for their
lives. It was a complete victory for Alfred and the
Anglo Saxons.

12 Guthrum, King of the defeated Viking army,
was received by King Alfred. To his great
surprise, he found that Alfred did not want revenge;
instead he treated Guthrum as a friend.

13 Guthrum, like all the Vikings, was not a Christian. King Alfred persuaded him to be baptised into the Christian faith and acted as his godfather.

14 Alfred and Guthrum agreed to divide England between them, as can be seen in this map. These Vikings were Danes from Denmark and the area given to them was known as the 'Danelaw'. Alfred took into Wessex, part of Mercia and the small kingdom of Kent. The two kings agreed to live as neighbours, in peace. But, as will be seen, the peace did not last very long

The Sea Rovers

While Alfred the Great was defending his kingdom, fleets of longships from Norway and Denmark were sweeping the coasts and driving up the rivers of Europe, burning and looting. This is the story of two famous Viking sea rovers, who spread havoc from the English Channel to the Mediterranean coasts.

1 Hastein and Bjorn Ironside, two swashbuckling Viking chiefs, led a fleet of longships up the River Seine, to Paris. They plundered the houses and churches and loaded their ships with treasure.

2 Having plundered Paris, the two chiefs decided to give the same treatment to an even greater city — Rome, in distant Italy. They set sail for the south with a great fleet of 62 ships.

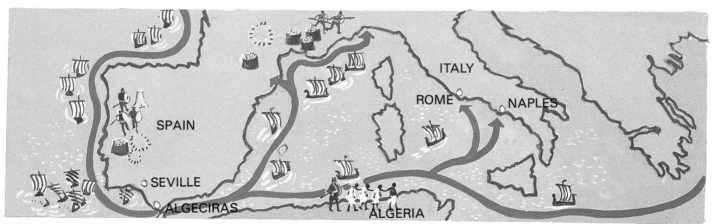

3 On the way south, they raided many small coastal towns.

The people of Seville, in Spain, were ready for the raiders. A Spanish fleet lay in wait for them and, in a fierce sea battle, the Vikings had to make off as quickly as they could. They were forced to leave two of their ships behind.

Passing through the Straits of Gibraltar, the Vikings plundered Algeciras.

They raided the North African coast, looking for Negro slaves.

All along the Mediterranean coast of France, they looted towns and carried off more treasure to load into their ships.

4 The story so far, is history — written down by people who were alive at the time. What follows is a good story — but may not all be true. It is said that, at the end of their long and eventful voyage, Hastein and Bjorn at last sighted a city built of white marble. It looked so splendid that they decided it must be Rome.

5 The walls of the city were far too strong to attack, so the Viking made a plan. They sent messages to the city to say that their chief was old and sick. He wanted to be baptised a Christian before he died. He begged to be allowed into the city.

6 The bishop of the city agreed to baptise Hastein, but on the following day, another messenger was sent to say that the chief had died in the night and his last request was to be given a Christian burial in the city cathedral. He was carried ashore in a coffin and taken to the cathedral.

7 But he was only pretending to be dead. As the funeral service began, Hastein sprang from the coffin and killed the bishop. His followers, drawing swords from beneath their mourning robes, dashed from the church.

8 Then, killing the guards, they opened the city gates for their armed shipmates.

9 Seeing that it was hopeless to resist, the city fathers surrendered. But the Vikings were in for a shock. It turned out that the place they had captured was a town called Luna — nearly 200 miles from Rome. It was the wrong city! The Vikings were furious when they discovered their mistake. They slaughtered the inhabitants and burned the city to the ground.

10 The Vikings, however, had to pay a high price for their cruelty. On their way back through the Straits of Gibraltar, they were attacked by a strong fleet from Spain. Out-numbered, the Vikings were badly beaten. Only twenty of the sixty-two ships that had set out four years earlier, returned safely. They had carried death and misery to thousands — but found their way into history.

Viking Britain — the end of the story

Of all the countries of Europe, England was the land most prized by the Vikings. It was a rich country with plunder to be found in the towns and land to farm in the countryside. When King Alfred died in 899 however, he left a strong Wessex, able to defend itself against further Viking attacks. He also built a navy to protect its coasts.

1 Within the Danelaw, the Viking invaders had settled down peacefully as farmers.

2 Across the Channel, in France, the King of France had also made peace with Viking invaders. Rollo, a Viking chieftain, was baptised and given Normandy (Northmen Land) to rule.

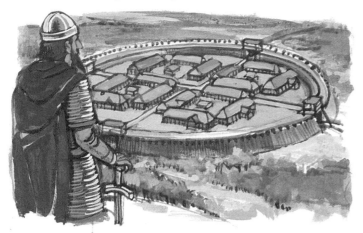

3 But then, after nearly one hundred years of peace, a new Viking threat arose. For the first time, a Danish king built military fortresses for a standing army. This was King Svein Forkbeard, who had decided to conquer England.

4 Faced with such a powerful threat, Ethelred, the English king, decided that fighting was useless. He paid the Vikings hundreds of silver pounds to persuade them to go away.

5 Svein Forkbeard took the money — and for a couple of years, kept the peace. But he used Ethelred's money to build up an even greater army. He launched another, more powerful attack on England — and King Ethelred escaped across the Channel.

6 Svein Forkbeard was accepted by the English people as their ruler. At last, after nearly a century of fighting, England had a Viking king!

7 That same year, Svein Forkbeard died and his son, Canute, became king. He was a wise ruler, treating all his subjects, English or Viking, in the same way. He was king, not only of all England, but of Norway and Denmark as well. When he was only 40 years old, he died and was buried in Winchester Cathedral.

8 The last Viking invasion took place in 1066. By now, no one could agree who should be king of England. An Englishman called Harold Godwinsson was crowned in Westminster Abbey, but at the same time, King Harald the Ruthless of Denmark was planning to seize the English throne for himself. Harald crossed the North Sea with a powerful Viking army and sailed up the River Ouse towards York.

9 Harold Godwinsson marched north at once, to challenge the invader. At Stamford Bridge, near York, a fierce battle was fought and Harald the Ruthless was killed.

10 But Harold Godwinsson's troubles were not over. While he was up in the North, another invasion had been launched. This time it was by the Duke of Normandy, who landed with his army at Hastings. He too wanted to be king of England.

11 The two sides met at Hastings in one of the most famous battles in English history. After a long struggle, the English were defeated. Harold is said to have been killed by an arrow which hit him in the eye.

12 William the Conqueror became King of England. His Viking ancestor, Rollo of Normandy, would have been very pleased to see him on the throne. But it was the end of the Viking Age, for there was no need any more for raiding and plundering. The Vikings had become respectable at last. They had become English!

Our Viking Heritage

The Vikings first attacked England in the year 793 when the monastery at Lindisfarne was plundered and the monks dispersed. Then they came in ever increasing numbers until King Alfred made peace and confined them to the Danelaw. For nearly 300 years they were a powerful influence, founding new market towns, teaching the Anglo Saxons new ways of administering the law and bringing their own special kind of art. They left their mark on England in many ways.

1 They left their mark on the language. What do these three things have in common? —

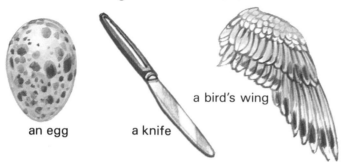

an egg   a knife   a bird's wing

they all have Viking names. Other Viking words are:

anger	die	them
awe	haven	there
bait	law	they
boon	sale	wand
crooked	take	wrong

NORTON BY TOFT 10   RESBY   7
KIRKBY 15   KINGTHORPE 14

2 All the names on this signpost are of places where Vikings lived in the Danelaw. They gave the place Danish names. Other Viking place names are:

-by, meaning farm or village
Coningsby — king's village
Denby — Danes' village
Derby — animal farm
Ingleby — village of the English
Normanby — village of the Norsemen
Selby — willow farm
Sowerby — muddy farm

-toft, meaning homestead

Lowestoft — Hlothver's homestead
Wigtoft — homestead on the creek
Bratoft — broad homestead
Nortoft — north homestead

-thwaite, meaning clearing, meadow or field
Braithwaite — broad clearing
Applethwaite — apple tree clearing
Brackenthwaite — bracken clearing
Kirkthwaite — church field

-thorpe, meaning hamlet or small village

Burythorpe — hill hamlet
Scunthorpe — Skuma's hamlet
Mablethorpe — Malbert's hamlet
Grassthorpe — grass hamlet

See if you can find more on a map of England

3 They left their mark on our customs and traditions. One example is in Cumberland, where men enjoy a kind of wrestling which was brought to England by the Vikings.

Jorvik

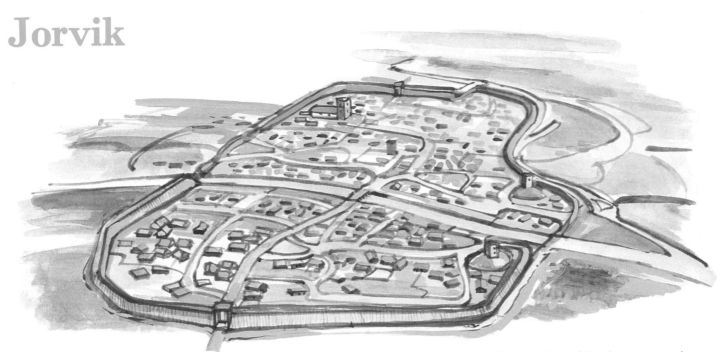

1 The Vikings also left their mark on our townlife, and many English towns were started or developed by the Vikings. One of the best examples is Jorvik (York) which was the biggest Viking settlement in Europe.

2 Many of the secrets of Jorvik have been uncovered by archaeologists. In 1976 they started to dig up the site of one of the old Viking streets, Coppergate.

3 As a result of their discoveries the Viking street of Coppergate has been reconstructed at the Jorvik Viking Centre. Special trolley cars carry visitors back in time into a world of Viking sights, smells and sounds.

Model of a Viking Longship

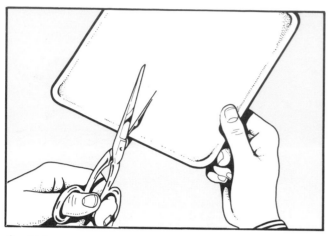

1   Take a plastic meat tray with deep sides. Cut it in half.

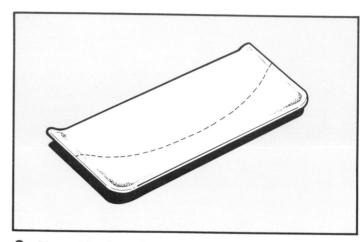

2   Draw this shape in one of the halves.

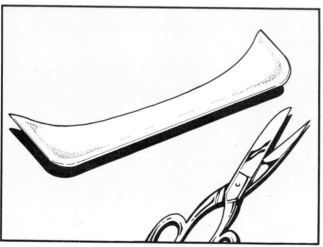

3   Cut out the shape. This will be one side of the ship.

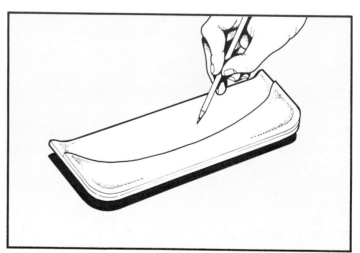

4   Fit the cut section into the other half of the tray and draw round it.

5   Cut out this shape from the spare plastic. This will be the ship's prow.

6   Use UHU glue to fix the two halves together to make the hull.

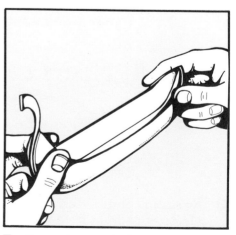

7   Press the two halves together and glue the section of prow between them like this.

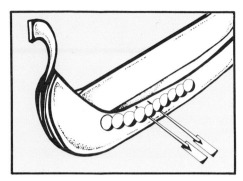

8 Press drawing pins into the side of the hull. These are the crew's shields. Push cocktail sticks into the sides of the hull to make oars. Stick a piece of card at the end of each oar to make blades.

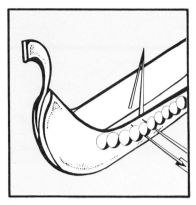

9 Press two cocktail sticks inside the ship to support the mast. Use another cocktail stick for the rudder.

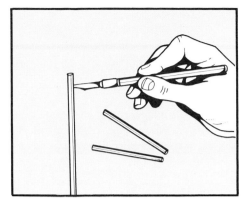

10 Take two plastic drinking straws. Make a slit down one of them. Cut the other in half to make a yard arm.

11 Cut a sheet of paper the width of the half-drinking straw. Trim it like this and glue it to the yard arm.

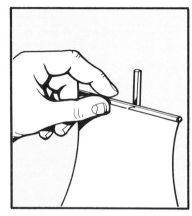

12 Fix a mapping pin into the middle of the yard arm and slide it down the slot in the mast.

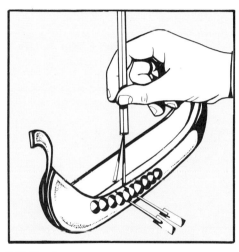

13 Fit the mast and sail over the two cocktail sticks inside the ship.

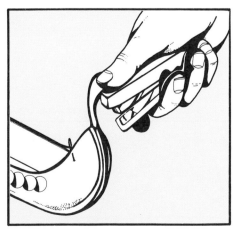

14 Use a wire stapler to make hooks along the side of the hull for the rigging lines.

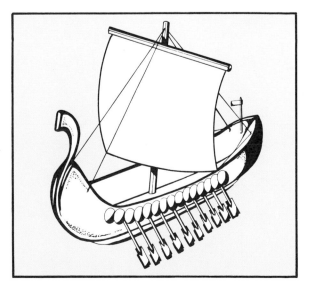

15 Rig the ship like this. Shirring thread (elasticated cotton) makes good rigging. If you stick some plasticine to the bottom of the hull for a keel, your Viking Longship will sail — but first put the oars inboard.

Index

Adventures, Viking, map of, 8 and 9
Alfred, king,
    and battle of Edington, 22
    and King Guthrum, 23
    burns the cakes, 22
    hides from the Danes, 21
Althing, parliament, 16
Anglo-Saxons, 20
Asgard, dwelling place of gods, 16
Bjarne, and discovery of America, 13
Bjorn, adventures, 24 and 25
Canute, King, 27
Cooking, implements for, 5
Craftsmen, Viking, 7
Cumberland wrestling, 28
Danelaw, 23
Denmark, description of, 4
Erik the Red, 12
Ethelred, king, 26
Farming, Vikings in Scandinavia, 5
Figurehead, on ship, 11
Fight ring, 12
Forkbeard, Svein, and England, 26
Giants, and Thor, 17 to 19
    and cat, 18 and 19
Gibraltar, Vikings at, 24 and 25
Greenland, first settlement at, 12
Gudrid,
    leaves Vinland, 15
    marries Karlsefni, 14
    rescue of, 13
    visits Rome, 15
Harald the Ruthless, king, 27
Harold Godwinsson, his death, 27
Hastein, adventures of, 24 and 25
Heindall, son of Odin, 16
Houses,
    farms, 5
    in towns, 6
Iceland,
    and Ingolfur, 11
    map of 8 and 9
    new church in, 15
    first settlement at, 11

Indians, in Vinland, 14
Ingolfur, in Iceland, 11
Italy, Viking attacks on, 24
Ivar the Boneless, and England, 20
Jorvik, Viking York, 29
Karlsefni, marries Gudrid, 14
Lindisfarne, monastery at, 2 and 3
Longships, 10 and 11
Luna, mistaken for Rome, 25
Mediterranean, Viking adventures in, 24
Midgard, and Thor, 18 and 19
Northumbria, and the Vikings, 20
Odin, Viking god, 16
Oseberg ship, 11
Paris, Viking attack on, 24
Reykjavik, in Iceland, 12
Rome, and Viking attacks, 24 and 25
Sagas, 12
Scandinavia,
    description of, 4
    map of, 4
Ships, of Vikings, 10 and 11
Ship, model of, 30 and 31
Shops, 7, 29
Thor, son of Odin, 16
    his journey, 17 to 19
Valhalla, 16
Valkyries, 16
Vinland, discovery of, 13
Vikings,
    adventures, 8 and 9
    attacks, on Lindisfarne, 2 and 3, on Paris, 24
    farmers, 4 and 5
    homeland of, 4
    in Mediterranean, 24 and 25
    place names in England, 28
    ships, 7, 10 and 11
    towns, 6
    words in English language, 28
York,
    falls to Ivar the Boneless, 20
    Viking excavations at, 29